FEB   2014

I C O N S

History Makers

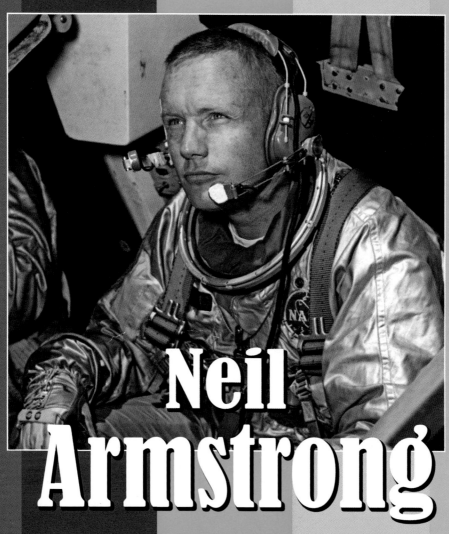

Neil
Armstrong

by Anita Yasuda

MEDIA ENHANCED BOOKS
AV²
BY WEIGL™
ADDED VALUE • AUDIO VISUAL

www.av2books.com

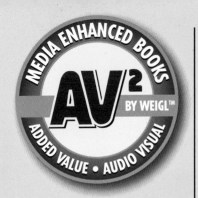

AV² provides enriched content that supplements and complements this book. Weigl's AV² books strive to create inspired learning and engage young minds in a total learning experience.

Your AV² Media Enhanced books come alive with...

Audio
Listen to sections of the book read aloud.

Key Words
Study vocabulary, and complete a matching word activity.

Video
Watch informative video clips.

Quizzes
Test your knowledge.

Embedded Weblinks
Gain additional information for research.

Slide Show
View images and captions, and prepare a presentation.

Try This!
Complete activities and hands-on experiments.

... and much, much more!

Go to **www.av2books.com**, and enter this book's unique code.

BOOK CODE

N214688

AV² by Weigl brings you media enhanced books that support active learning.

Published by AV² by Weigl
350 5th Avenue, 59th Floor
New York, NY 10118

www.av2books.com   www.weigl.com

Library of Congress Cataloging-in-Publication Data

Yasuda, Anita.
Neil Armstrong / Anita Yasuda.
    p. cm. -- (Remarkable people)
Audience: 4-6.
 Summary: A biography of the first man on the moon, covering his youth and his career as an astronaut.
 Includes index.
 ISBN 978-1-62127-304-2 (hardcover : alk. paper) -- ISBN 978-1-62127-310-3 (softcover : alk. paper)
1. Armstrong, Neil, 1930-2012--Juvenile literature. 2. Astronauts--United States--Biography--Juvenile literature. I. Title.
 TL789.85.A75Y37 2014
 629.450092--dc23
 [B]
                    2013000833

Printed in the United States of America in North Mankato, Minnesota
1 2 3 4 5 6 7 8 9 0   17 16 15 14 13

WEP040413
052013

Editor: Megan Cuthbert
Design: Tammy West

Photograph Credits
Weigl acknowledges Getty Images as the primary image supplier for this title. Every reasonable effort has been made to trace ownership and to obtain permission to reprint copyright material. The publishers would be pleased to have any errors or omissions brought to their attention so that they may be corrected in subsequent printings.

Contents

Who Was Neil Armstrong?

O n July 20, 1969, astronaut Neil Armstrong became the first person to walk on the Moon. Almost 530 million people watched when *Apollo 11*'s **lunar module**, The Eagle, landed on the Moon. Climbing down from the capsule, Neil said, "That's one small step for man, one giant leap for mankind."

When Neil returned to Earth, he was a celebrity. People were excited that the *Apollo 11* mission was a success. They considered Neil a hero. In New York City, four million people came out to celebrate the *Apollo 11* astronauts in a massive parade. According to one report, the air was so thick with confetti that the astronauts could barely see.

"*Mystery creates wonder and wonder is the basis for man's desire to understand.*"

Growing Up

Neil Alden Armstrong was born August 5, 1930 near Wapakoneta, Ohio. Neil's father, Stephen, was an auditor for the state of Ohio. His job required many moves. The Armstrongs moved 16 times before Neil graduated from high school.

Neil's mother, Viola, worked at a local department store before marrying Stephen. After marriage, Viola took care of the family. Neil was the eldest child. His sister, June Louise, was born in 1933, and his brother, Dean Alan, was born in 1935.

Neil's father first introduced him to airplanes at the age of two when they attended the National Air Races in Cleveland. This was the beginning of a lifelong interest in flight. Soon after, Neil convinced his mother to buy him a toy plane. He played with the plane endlessly.

▲ The National Air Races began in 1920 and traveled to several American cities before settling in Cleveland in 1929.

Get to Know
Ohio

LAKE ERIE

SCALE

0   75 Miles

0   75 Kilometers

OHIO

INDIANA

PENNSYLVANIA

WEST VIRGINIA

Neil Armstrong's birth city, Wapakoneta, is home to the Armstrong Air & Space Museum.

Ohio is known as the birthplace of aviation. It was home to aviation pioneers, the Wright brothers, who experimented with and built many piloted flying machines.

STATE SYMBOLS

TREE
Ohio Buckeye

BIRD
Cardinal

Agriculture is Ohio's largest industry, with corn and soybeans being the top products.

FLOWER
Red Carnation

Columbus is the capital of Ohio.

Practice Makes Perfect

When Neil was six years old, his father took him to the airport in Warren, Ohio. He wanted to give Neil a new experience, and the airport was offering airplane rides for 25 cents. The plane they boarded was a Ford Tri-motor plane. While Neil's father found the rattling plane nerve-wracking, Neil loved it. By the time he was eight, Neil knew he wanted to be an aircraft designer.

Neil spent hours making model airplanes. He also read everything he could about airplanes. Magazines such as *Flight, Air Trails,* and *Model Airplane News* fascinated him.

▲ The Ford Tri-motor was the first airplane designed for the purpose of carrying passengers. The plane had three engines, which made it very loud.

In high school, Neil excelled in the sciences. He especially enjoyed physics. His teacher, John Crites, encouraged students to do special projects. Neil built a **wind tunnel**, just like the Wright brothers did when they were younger.

Outside of school, Neil took flying lessons. He thought a good aircraft designer should also be a pilot. Neil was one of the youngest students in the class. In order to pay for lessons, he worked at the local drug store. He had to work many hours just to afford one flying lesson. Neil's hard work paid off. He earned his pilot's license before he could even drive a car. Neil was only 16.

QUICK FACTS

- **Asteroid** 6469 Armstrong is named after Neil Armstrong.

- Neil Armstrong and fellow *Apollo 11* astronaut, Edwin 'Buzz' Aldrin, left behind a plaque on the Moon. It said "We came in peace for all mankind."

- Neil was in the **Korean War** and flew 78 combat missions.

◀ On December 17, 1903, Orville Wright flew the *Wright Flyer* for 12 seconds over a total length of 120 feet (37 meters). It was the first time an aircraft had achieved sustained flight while being piloted.

Key Events

Neil enrolled at Purdue University, and studied **aeronautical engineering**. After completing his degree, Neil began work for the **National Advisory Committee for Aeronautics (NACA)**. He worked as both a research pilot and a research engineer. Neil piloted a variety of cutting edge **hypersonic** planes. One of these planes was the X-15. Flights aboard this rocket-powered aircraft took Neil to the edge of space. He realized that, if he wanted to fly in outer space, he would have to become an astronaut.

In 1962, the National Aeronautics and Space Administration (NASA) accepted Neil into the astronaut training program. Now, he would have the opportunity to fly into space. Four years later, NASA chose Neil to command the *Gemini 8* mission, with his co-pilot, David Scott. Neil and David made history when they docked their *Gemini 8* spacecraft with the rocket *Agena*. Two spacecraft had never connected in **orbit** before.

Back on Earth, Neil worked on other NASA projects. He used **simulators** to practice a lunar landing. He also tested lunar landing vehicles. Neil would get the chance to use this knowledge as commander of *Apollo 11*.

◀ As command pilot for the *Gemini 8* mission, Neil Armstrong became the first person who was not from the military to fly a U.S. spacecraft. His co-pilot, David Scott, had served in the Air Force.

Thoughts from Neil

Neil was grateful for the opportunities he had been given. Here are a few of his comments on public life, NASA, and the space program.

Neil talks about the perception that he stayed out of the public eye.

"... from my perspective it doesn't seem that way, because I do so many things, I go so many places, I give so many talks...I'm only able to accept less than one percent of all the requests..."

Neil describes the Moon.

"It's a brilliant surface in that sunlight... It's an interesting place to be. I recommend it."

Neil talks about what he would like to be remembered for.

"I guess we all like to be recognized not for one piece of fireworks, but for the ledger of our daily work."

Neil explains what people thought of space travel in the 1950s.

"...in those days space flight was not generally regarded as a realistic objective... So although we were working toward that end, it was not something that we acknowledged much publicly."

Neil talks about his experiences as a pilot.

"Gliders, sail planes, they're wonderful flying machines. It's the closest you can come to being a bird."

Neil talks about NASA's decision to send people to the Moon.

"...put men, a crew on it, not just take it into orbit, to take it to the Moon, it seemed incredibly aggressive. But we were for it. We thought that was a wonderful opportunity."

What Is an Astronaut?

Astronauts are highly educated men and women. They often have backgrounds in engineering, medicine, or science. It is quite common for astronauts to have experience as military pilots, like Neil Armstrong. Besides having the necessary technical training, astronauts must be able to get along with others. This will help them when they have to work in small, cramped stations and ships. Astronauts come from all over the world. Once chosen for an astronaut training program, candidates must prove that they are physically fit.

At the Johnson Space Center in Houston, Texas, candidates study a wide range of subjects, from parachute jumping to mathematics and science. If candidates complete this program, they earn the title 'astronaut.' They can then go on to more advanced training. Becoming an astronaut takes years of hard work and dedication. Astronauts work long hours and must be willing to spend long periods away from family and friends.

▶ Astronauts often have to participate in media events surrounding their missions, such as being photographed and taking part in press conferences.

NASA

NASA was officially established in 1958 by President Dwight Eisenhower. The program was a continuation of NACA. NACA had studied flight technology for the previous 40 years. Now, NASA would focus on using flight technology in space. Although NASA is best known for taking astronauts into space, the program also aims to improve flight technology and conduct scientific research. This research is used to gain a better understanding of Earth, the solar system, and the universe.

Astronauts 101

John Glenn (1921–)

John Glenn was born on July 18, 1921, in Cambridge, Ohio. He was a military pilot and fought in both World War II and the Korean War. As a U.S. Navy test pilot, John set a speed record from Los Angeles to New York. In 1959, he started astronaut training. He was the first American to orbit Earth, on the *Friendship 7* rocket ship. John returned to space at the age of 77 aboard the shuttle *Discovery*. He received the **Presidential Medal of Freedom** in 2012.

Alan B. Shepard, Jr. (1923–1998)

Alan B. Shepard, Jr. was born on November 18, 1923 in East Derry, New Hampshire. Alan studied at the U.S. Naval Academy and fought in World War II. When the war ended, Alan went to the Navy Test Pilot School in Maryland. In 1959, Alan was accepted into NASA's program for space exploration. On May 5, 1961 Alan became the first American in space, aboard the *Freedom 7*. His journey lasted 15 minutes. Alan went back into space in 1971, where he became the fifth person to walk on the Moon.

Sally Ride (1951–2012)

Sally Ride was born in Los Angeles, California, on May 26, 1951. She completed her astronaut training in 1979 and became the **mission specialist** on *STS-7* in 1983. Sally was the first American woman in space. She returned to space in 1984. After leaving NASA, Sally worked as a physics professor at the University of San Diego and as the director of the California Space Institute. In 2001, she founded Sally Ride Science, a company that motivates girls to pursue careers in science and technology.

Dr. Mae C. Jemison (1956–)

Mae is a scientist, physician, teacher, and astronaut. She was born on October 17, 1956, in Decatur, Alabama. Mae attended Stanford University and graduated in 1977. She went on to earn a doctorate in medicine from Cornell University. In 1987, she was selected for the NASA astronaut program. She joined space shuttle *Endeavour*'s team in 1992 as the science mission specialist. She was the first African American woman to go into space. Today, Mae is working on a satellite-based telecommunication system to improve health care in West Africa.

Influences

Neil's earliest influences were his mother and father. Viola and Stephen Armstrong worked hard to provide Neil with the experiences and opportunities to reach his dreams. Viola was too worried to watch Neil fly, but she did not stop him from doing it. Neil was always confident. He never showed the slightest fear.

Growing up, Neil had many aviation heroes, including Canadian World War I flying ace Billy Bishop. Neil thought that World War I pilots were very brave. Neil also admired record setters such as Charles Lindbergh. Charles made the first non-stop solo flight across the Atlantic Ocean in 1927.

◀ **Charles Lindbergh completed his trans-Atlantic flight onboard a plane named "Spirit of St. Louis." The entire flight took 33 hours and 30 minutes.**

At the local Wapakoneta airport, Neil took flight instruction from three veteran army pilots. In order to practice, Neil would ride his bike miles to the strip. When Neil was not in the air, he liked to talk to World War II veterans who had plenty of flying experience. He enjoyed listening to their stories and absorbed their knowledge like a sponge. By the age of 17, Neil had completed two cross-country solo flights.

THE ARMSTRONG FAMILY

Neil married his first wife, Janet Shearon, in 1956. They met at Purdue University. The couple had three children. Eric was born in 1957, followed by Karen in 1959, and Mark in 1963. Sadly, Karen died when she was only 3 years old. Neil and Janet divorced in 1994. Neil married Carol Held Knight the same year.

▲ Neil's oldest son, Eric, was only 12 years old when his father first stepped on the Moon.

Overcoming Obstacles

Neil's journey from small town boy to commander of *Apollo 11* took years of hard work, dedication, and courage. While he was studying at Purdue University, Neil served time in the Navy. Although Neil had a pilot's license, he had only flown single-engine planes. Neil was plunged into intense Navy pilot training in preparation for the Korean War. He had to master many skills, including learning to land on an aircraft carrier. During the war, a cable booby-trap sliced off part of his plane's wing. Neil parachuted to safety.

As command pilot of *Gemini 8*, Neil faced danger again. After docking with the *Agena* rocket, both crafts began to tumble. The ships were spinning so fast that the astronauts could not see properly and almost lost consciousness. Neil remained calm. He stopped the spacecraft from rolling and restored stability.

◀ The *Gemini 8* mission had to perform an emergency re-entry back to Earth after the spacecraft began to roll uncontrollably. As a result, the entire mission could not be completed.

In the 1960s, the United States was in a race against the **Soviet Union** to put the first person on the Moon. At the height of the **space race**, NASA chose Neil as commander of *Apollo 11*. As commander, he would face the biggest challenges of his life. Neil and his fellow astronauts prepared for the Moon landing for years. Landing the untested lunar module would be hard enough, but no one knew if the rockets would bring the astronauts home. On July 16, 1969, *Apollo 11* blasted off from Florida's Kennedy Space Center, with Neil Armstrong, Edwin 'Buzz' Aldrin, and Michael Collins onboard. Neil used his skills and training to make the lunar mission a success. On July 20, 1969, the lunar module landed safely on the Moon.

▶ The *Apollo 11* spacecraft was launched into space by the Saturn V rocket, which was 363 feet (111 meters) tall.

Achievements and Successes

It was not until *Apollo 11* returned safely to Earth on July 24, 1969, that the mission was declared a complete success. Following their homecoming, the astronauts went on a worldwide tour. It took them to 24 cities. Neil and his crewmates received the Presidential Medal of Freedom. NASA honored Neil's contributions to the space program with the NASA Distinguished Service Medal.

In 2011, Neil Armstrong, Buzz Aldrin, and Michael Collins travelled to Washington, D.C. The United States Congress presented them with the New Frontier Congressional Gold Medal. The medal recognized their historic achievement.

◀ A massive ticker tape parade was held in New York City on August 13, 1969 to celebrate the *Apollo 11* astronauts. Parades were also held in Chicago, Los Angeles, and Mexico City.

Neil was proud of *Apollo 11*'s achievements, but he did not enjoy being in the spotlight. Neil felt he was just doing his job. After leaving NASA, Neil quietly worked as a professor of aerospace engineering at the University of Cincinnati.

On August 25, 2012, Neil Armstrong died. A tribute was held in his honor at the Washington National Cathedral. It was attended by many of Neil's former crewmates and fellow astronauts.

HELPING OTHERS

Astronauts like Neil Armstrong sometimes use their celebrity to increase public awareness of issues they care about. They may bring attention to environmental problems or organizations that are helping others. Sometimes, the family of a well-known figure like Neil will set up memorial funds. The Neil Armstrong New Frontiers Initiative is a children's health fund in his memory. Neil's legacy supports research at the Cincinatti Children's Hospital Medical Center. The Neil Armstrong Scholarship Fund at the Telluride Foundation was also established in Neil's honor. Telluride was where Neil had a second home for many years. Neil's fund provides scholarships to students who are pursuing studies in mathematics, science, engineering, or technology.

▶ **Neil spent many years as a motivational speaker. He traveled around the world, talking about his experiences as an astronaut.**

Write a Biography

A person's life story can be the subject of a book. This kind of book is called a biography. Biographies describe the lives of remarkable people, such as those who have achieved great success or have done important things to help others. These people may be alive today, or they may have lived many years ago. Reading a biography can help you learn more about a remarkable person.

At school, you might be asked to write a biography. First, decide who you want to write about. You can choose an astronaut, such as Neil Armstrong, or any other person. Then, find out if your library has any books about this person. Learn as much as you can about him or her. Write down the key events in this person's life. What was this person's childhood like? What has he or she accomplished? What are his or her goals? What makes this person special or unusual?

A concept web is a useful research tool. Read the questions in the following concept web. Answer the questions in your notebook. Your answers will help you write a biography.

Writing a Biography

Your Opinion
- What did you learn from the books you read in your research?
- Would you suggest these books to others?
- Was anything missing from these books?

Childhood
- Where and when was this person born?
- Describe his or her parents, siblings, and friends.
- Did this person grow up in unusual circumstances?

Adulthood
- Where does this individual currently reside?
- Does he or she have a family?

Main Accomplishments
- What is this person's life's work?
- Has he or she received awards or recognition for accomplishments?
- How have this person's accomplishments served others?

Work and Preparation
- What was this person's education?
- What was his or her work experience?
- How does this person work; what is or was the process he or she uses or used?

Help and Obstacles
- Did this individual have a positive attitude?
- Did he or she receive help from others?
- Did this person have a mentor?
- Did this person face any hardships?
- If so, how were the hardships overcome?

Timeline

YEAR	NEIL ARMSTRONG	WORLD EVENTS
1930	Neil Alden Armstrong is born near Wapakoneta, Ohio.	Pluto is discovered.
1955	After serving in the Korean War, Neil returns to university where he earns an aeronautical engineering degree.	The Baikonur Cosmodrome, a missile and space test center for the Soviet Union, is founded in Kazakhstan.
1962	Neil becomes one of nine men chosen for the NASA astronaut program.	John Glenn becomes the first American to orbit Earth.
1966	Neil, commander of *Gemini 8*, becomes the first person not from the military to command a spacecraft.	The Soviet Union lands the unmanned *Luna 9* on the Moon.
1969	Neil becomes the first man to walk on the Moon.	Richard M. Nixon becomes the 37th president of the United States.
1986	After the Space Shuttle *Challenger* explodes following takeoff, Neil serves on the presidential commission investigating the accident.	The Rutan Model 76 Voyager is the first airplane to complete a nonstop flight around the world.
2012	Neil dies on August 25 in Cincinnati, Ohio.	Barack Obama is elected for a second term as president of the United States.

Key Words

aeronautical engineering: the design, science, and construction of aircraft

asteroid: a rock that orbits the Sun

hypersonic: something that is traveling more than five times the speed of sound

Korean War: a war fought from 1950 to 1953 between communists and non-communist forces

lunar module: a manned vehicle for use outside of a spacecraft

mission specialist: an astronaut assigned to a specific task during a space mission

National Advisory Committee for Aeronautics (NACA): an agency formed in 1915 to study, research, and improve flight technology

orbit: the path a spacecraft takes as it moves around a heavenly body

Presidential Medal of Freedom: the highest civilian award in the United States

simulators: programs or machines designed to recreate a situation or environment so that people can practice and learn

Soviet Union: also known as the Union of Soviet Socialist Republics (USSR), it was a union of countries that existed between 1921 and 1991

space race: a competition between the United States and the Soviet Union to be the dominant country in space exploration

wind tunnel: a large tube-like tunnel used to test how an aircraft will fly

Index

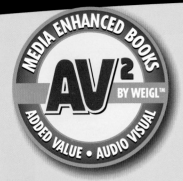

Log on to www.av2books.com

AV² by Weigl brings you media enhanced books that support active learning. Go to www.av2books.com, and enter the special code found on page 2 of this book. You will gain access to enriched and enhanced content that supplements and complements this book. Content includes video, audio, weblinks, quizzes, a slide show, and activities.

AV² Online Navigation

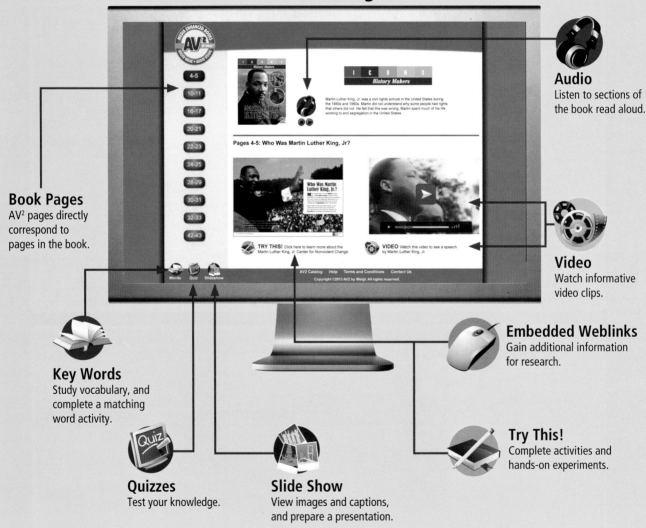

Audio
Listen to sections of the book read aloud.

Book Pages
AV² pages directly correspond to pages in the book.

Video
Watch informative video clips.

Key Words
Study vocabulary, and complete a matching word activity.

Embedded Weblinks
Gain additional information for research.

Try This!
Complete activities and hands-on experiments.

Quizzes
Test your knowledge.

Slide Show
View images and captions, and prepare a presentation.

AV² was built to bridge the gap between print and digital. We encourage you to tell us what you like and what you want to see in the future.

Sign up to be an AV² Ambassador at www.av2books.com/ambassador.

Due to the dynamic nature of the Internet, some of the URLs and activities provided as part of AV² by Weigl may have changed or ceased to exist. AV² by Weigl accepts no responsibility for any such changes. All media enhanced books are regularly monitored to update addresses and sites in a timely manner. Contact AV² by Weigl at 1-866-649-3445 or av2books@weigl.com with any questions, comments, or feedback.